WHY THE OLD COVENANT FAILED

Some time ago I stepped off the platform at the close of an evangelistic message and hurried toward the front door to greet the people. Suddenly my path was blocked by three young men, one of whom addressed me in quite a loud voice. He said, "Brother Joe, we were disappointed with the way you put us back under the Old Covenant tonight by preaching the seventh-day Sabbath. Don't you realize that we are living under the New Covenant now and should be keeping Sunday instead of the Sabbath?"

That young man was voicing the conviction of many thousands of Christians today who sincerely believe that the Ten Commandments constituted the Old Covenant, which disappeared at the cross and, therefore, has no present application to grace-saved Christians. Is it a true premise? If so, we certainly need to be clearly apprised of the doctrine in order to avoid the pitfall of deadly legalism. On the other hand, if the Ten Commandments are still binding, it would be the most tragic mistake to discount even one of those great moral precepts.

No one can deny that there are Old Testament statements which refer to the Ten Commandments as a covenant; however, it will be our purpose here to show that the Ten-Commandment law was *not* the Old Covenant which was abolished.

But before we delve into this fascinating subject, we need to define what a covenant really is. There are many types and forms, but basically a covenant is an agreement between two parties based upon mutual promises. All through the centuries God has dealt with His people on the basis of covenants. He is a reasonable God, and he invites, "Come now, and let us reason together." Isaiah 1:18.

Sometimes God established pacts with individuals like Moses, Abraham, and David, and sometimes with the nation of Israel. The most important covenant of all was set up long before this world came into existence. It was a covenant between the Father and the Son and had to do with the eventuality of sin. Jesus offered Himself there in the vast eternity of the past as the "Lamb slain from the foundation of the world." Revelation 13:8. He agreed to become the atoning sacrifice to redeem man, should Adam and Eve choose to sin.

The terms of that eternal covenant have never been changed or superseded. Although many other covenants have been established through the years, the simple provision of salvation through faith has remained in effect through all ages, for all mankind.

The covenant which has caused the most misunderstanding, though, is designated as "the Old Covenant" by the writer of Hebrews. He also describes the institution of a new covenant which has some very important advantages over the old. Here is how he describes the two: "But now hath he obtained a more excellent ministry, by how much also he is the mediator of a better covenant, which was established upon better promises. For if that first covenant had been faultless, then should no place have been sought for the second. For finding fault with them, he saith, Behold, the days come, saith the Lord, when I will make a new covenant with the house of Israel and with the house of Judah: Not according to the covenant that I made with their fathers in the day when I took them by the hand to lead them out of the land of Egypt; because they continued not in my covenant, and I regarded them not, saith the Lord. For this is the covenant that I will make with the house of Israel after those days, saith the Lord; I will put my laws into their mind, and write them in their hearts: and I will be to them a God, and they shall be to me a people: ... For I will be merciful to their unrighteousness, and their sins and their iniquities will I remember no more. In that he saith, A new covenant, he hath made the first old. Now that which decayeth and waxeth old is ready to vanish away." Hebrews 8:6-13.

This description leaves no room for doubt concerning the fate of the Old Covenant. It was set aside in favor of a new one which had better promises. Naturally, we are interested to know all about that new covenant which will place God's law in the heart and mind. But we also need to understand the nature of the covenant which disappeared. Millions have been taught that it was the Ten-Commandment law. They boast of being delivered from the law and claim to walk in a glorious freedom from the Old Testament covenant of works.

The Old Covenant—
Not the Ten Commandments

Is this a biblical position? It is just as important to understand what the Old Covenant was not, as to know what it was.

Right now, let us look at three absolute proofs that the covenant which disappeared was not the Ten Commandments. Then we will determine by comparing scripture with scripture just what the Old Covenant was.

First of all, we notice that the Old Covenant had some poor promises in it. The New Covenant, we are told, "was established upon better promises." Verse 6. Tell me, has anyone ever been able to point out any poor promises in the Ten Commandments? Never. On the contrary, Paul declares that they were very good. "Children, obey your parents in the Lord: for this is right. Honour thy father and mother; which is the first commandment with promise; That it may be well with thee, and thou mayest live long on the earth." Ephesians 6:1-3.

This declaration alone is sufficient to show that the writer of Hebrews was not charging the moral law with any weak promises. The Old Covenant, whatever else it might be, could never be the Ten Commandments.

The second thing wrong with the Old

Covenant was that it was faulty. The Bible says, "For if that first covenant had been faultless, then should no place have been sought for the second." Hebrews 8:7. Let me ask you a question: Has any man ever been able to find a fault or a flaw in the handwriting of God? The psalmist declared, "The law of the Lord is perfect, converting the soul." Psalm 19:7. Paul wrote, "Wherefore the law is holy, and the commandment holy, and just, and good." Romans 7:12.

Does that sound like something weak and imperfect? No law could be perfect and faulty at the same time. It becomes more and more apparent that the Old Covenant could not have been the Ten Commandments.

Finally, though, we read the most dramatic thing about the Old Covenant—it was to be abolished! "In that he saith, A new covenant, he hath made the first old. Now that which decayeth and waxeth old is ready to vanish away." Hebrews 8:13. Now we can ask a serious question that should settle every doubt on this matter. Did the great moral law of Ten Commandments vanish away? Anyone who has read the New Testament must answer, Absolutely not. Paul affirms the exact opposite about the law. He asked, "Do we then make void the law through faith? God forbid: yea, we establish the law." Romans 3:31.

Does the Bible contradict itself? Can something vanish away and be established at the same time? Did the same writer say opposite things about the same law? Just to be certain that Paul was not saying that the Old Covenant was the law, let us insert the words "Old Covenant" instead of the word "law" into Romans 3:31. "Do we than make void the Old Covenant through faith? God forbid: yea, we establish the Old Covenant."

That doesn't sound right at all, does it? We know that the Old Covenant had vanished away and could never be spoken of in this way. Very clearly, then, we can see that the covenant which came to an end could not have been the Ten Commandments.

What Was the Old Covenant?

Having found what the Old Covenant was not, we are now ready to identify it specifically from the Word. To do so we must go back in the Bible to the book of Exodus. Many people have failed to see that there was more than one covenant involved at Mt. Sinai. God called Moses up into the mountain *before* He gave the law and proposed a covenant between Him and His people: "And Moses went up unto God, and the Lord called unto him out of the mountain, saying, Thus shalt thou say to the house of Jacob, and tell the children of Israel; ... if ye will obey my voice indeed, and keep my covenant, then ye shall be a peculiar treasure unto me above all people: for all the earth is mine: And ye shall be unto me ... an holy nation. These are the words which thou shalt speak unto the children of Israel." Exodus 19:3-6.

Notice how God asked Moses to present His offer to the people. Here are all the elements of a true covenant. Conditions and promises are laid down for both sides.

If the children of Israel accept God's proposal, a covenant will be established. How did they respond to the divine offer? "And Moses came and called for the elders of the people, and laid before their faces all these words which the Lord commanded him. And all the people answered together, and said, All that the Lord hath spoken we will do.   And Moses returned the words of the people unto the Lord." Exodus 19:7, 8.

Just as soon as that answer went back to God, the basis for the Old Covenant was set up. But before it could go into formal operation there had to be a sealing or ratifying of the pact. This ritualistic service involved the sprinkling of the blood of an ox on the people and is described in Exodus 24:4-8: "And Moses wrote all the words of the Lord, and rose up early in the morning, and builded an altar under the hill, and twelve pillars, according to the twelve tribes of Israel. And he sent young men of the children of Israel which ... sacrificed peace offerings of oxen unto the Lord. And Moses took half of the blood, and put it in basins; and half of the blood he sprinkled on the altar. And he took the book of the covenant, and read in the audience of the people: and they said, All that the Lord hath said will we do, and be obedient. And Moses took the blood, and sprinkled it on the people, and said, Behold the blood of the covenant, which the Lord hath made with you concerning all these words."

Again we are reminded that this covenant was not the law itself but was made "concerning all these words." The Ten Commandments were the basis for the agreement. The people promised to keep that law, and God promised to bless them in return. The crucial weakness in the whole arrangement revolved around the way Israel promised. There was no suggestion that they could not fully conform to every requirement of God. Neither was there any application for divine assistance. "We can do it," they insisted. Here is a perfect example of leaning on the flesh and trusting human strength. The words are filled with self-confidence. "All that the Lord hath said will we do, and be obedient."

Were they able to keep that promise? In

spite of their repeated assurances, they miserably broke their word before Moses could even get off the mountain with the tables of stone. Do we begin to see where the poor promises lay in the Old Covenant?

The book of Hebrews begins to unfold. There God is reported as "finding fault with them." Hebrews 8:8. He said, "Because they continued not in my covenant ... I regarded them not." Verse 9. The blame is placed squarely upon the human side of the mutual pact. Thus, we can see exactly why Paul wrote as he did about this Old Covenant in Hebrews 8. It did gender to bondage, it proved faulty, had poor promises, and vanished away—all because the people failed to obey their part of the agreement. Putting all these things together we can see why a new covenant was desperately needed, which would have better promises.

How were the New Covenant promises better? Because God made them, and they guaranteed successful obedience through His strength alone. "I will put my laws into their mind ... I will be to them a God ... I will be merciful to their unrighteousness, and their sins and their iniquities will I remember no more." Hebrews 8:10-12.

How was the New Covenant ratified? In the same manner that the Old was confirmed—by the shedding of blood. But instead of an ox having to shed its blood, the sinless Son of God would provide the blood of sprinkling: "Now the God of peace, that brought again from the dead our Lord Jesus, that great shepherd of the sheep, through the blood of the everlasting covenant, Make you perfect in every good work to do his will, working in you that which is well-pleasing in his sight, through Jesus Christ." Hebrews 13:20, 21.

What a contrast to the weak promises of the flesh made by Israel at Sinai. Instead of the people's "we will do," God's New Covenant promise is to "make you perfect in every good work ... working in you." It is no longer human effort. It is not so much you working, but Him "working in you." And how is this power made available? "Through the blood of the everlasting covenant." Because of what Jesus did on the cross.

The New Covenant
Based On Conversion

This brings us to the very heart of the New Covenant operation. Obedience is made possible by the writing of God's law on the heart. Through spiritual regeneration the mind and heart are transformed. Christ actually enters into the life of the believer and imparts His own strength for obedience. By partaking of the divine nature, the weakest human being begins to live the very life of Jesus Christ, manifesting His victory, and crucifying the flesh.

Paul describes that transaction this way: "For what the law could not do, in that it was weak through the flesh, God sending his own Son in the likeness of sinful flesh, and for sin, condemned sin in the flesh: That the righteousness of the law might be fulfilled in us, who walk not after the flesh, but after the Spirit." Romans 8:3, 4.

The word for righteousness is "dikaima," meaning "just requirement" of the law. In other words, because of Jesus' sinless life in the flesh, the requirement of the law can be fulfilled in us. He overcame sin in the same kind of body we have, so that He could impart that victory to us. He will actually live out His own holy life of separation from sin in our earthly bodies if we will permit Him to do so. This is the New Covenant promise for every believing, trusting child of God. And it is absolutely the only way that anyone can meet the requirements of the law: "Christ in you, the hope of glory." Colossians 1:27. "The life which I now live in the flesh I live by the faith of the Son of God, who loved me, and gave himself for me." Galatians 2:20.

It is most important for us to understand that the New Covenant law written on the heart is exactly the same law that was graven on the stone. Those great spiritual principles reflect the very character of God, and form the basis for His government.   The difference is not in the law but in the ministration of the law. Written only upon the tables of stone, they can only condemn and minister death, "because the carnal mind ... is not subject to the law of God." Romans 8:7. Received into the heart which has been spiritualized by the converting grace of Christ, the same law becomes a delight. The beloved John declared, "For this is the love of God, that we keep his commandments: and his commandments are not grievous." 1 John 5:3. Not only is the law not grievous for the Spirit-filled child of God, but obedience becomes a joyful possibility. The psalmist wrote, "I delight to do thy will, O my God: yea, thy law is within my heart." Psalms 40:8.

No Change in the
New Covenant After Calvary

Since the New Covenant was ratified by the blood of Christ, it obviously could not have gone into effect until after Jesus died on the cross. This crucial fact must not be overlooked. Eternal life or death could hinge upon the proper understanding of this key point. Paul wrote, "For where a testament is, there must also of necessity be the death of the testator. For a testament is of force after men are dead: otherwise it is of no strength at all while the testator liveth."

Hebrews 9:16, 17. The word "testament" is the same as the word "covenant." Only after a man's last will and testament has been ratified by his death can the provisions be executed. In the same way, Christ's covenant or testament would begin to operate just as soon as He had confirmed the covenant by His death at Calvary.

Another text leaves no question on this issue: "Brethren, I speak after the manner of men; Though it be but a man's covenant, yet if it be confirmed, no man disannulleth, or addeth thereto." Galatians 3:15. Paul is saying here that after a man's death, his will or covenant cannot be changed. Not one new addition can be made after the death of the testator. The covenant stands forever exactly as it stood when the testator died. After the death of Christ, no change whatsoever could be made in His provisions to save mankind. The conditions were all sealed and ratified by the shedding of blood. Every requirement had been laid down clearly by the perfect pattern of His sinless life and provision had been made for the writing of His magnified law, by the Holy

Spirit, upon the mind of each believer.

Under the terms of that New Covenant not one soul would be left to struggle helplessly against the powerful urges of a fallen nature. "Where sin abounded, grace did much more abound." Romans 5:20. Eternal promises rooted in the changeless nature of God would provide power to overcome every inherited and cultivated weakness. No wonder the Bible emphasizes the "better promises" of this glorious new agreement!

Now it is easy to understand some of the things Jesus did just before He died. For example, why did He institute the Lord's Supper before His body had been broken? On the Thursday night before His agonizing death on Friday, Jesus met with His disciples in that upper room. Holding the cup in His hands, He said, "This is my blood of the new testament, which is shed for many for the remission of sins." Matthew 26:28.

Isn't it curious that Christ would say those words before His blood had been shed? He was commanding a memorial for an event which had not even happened yet! Why?

Because it had to be introduced before His death in order to come under the New Covenant. Nothing could be added after His death.

Now, let me come back to the story I started to tell at the beginning of the book. I had just finished preaching on the subject of the Sabbath in one of my evangelistic crusades. As I stepped off the platform to greet the people as they left, three young men blocked my way in the aisle. One of them addressed me in quite a loud voice— loud enough to cause about fifty people near the front of the auditorium to stop and listen.

"Brother Joe," he said, "we were disappointed tonight with the way you put us back under the Old Covenant. Don't you realize that we are living under the New Covenant now, and should keep Sunday instead of the Sabbath?"

Although most of the congregation were leaving the building, the group near the front gathered closer to hear all that the young men were saying. It was obvious that I would have to take the time to answer this trio's challenging question. As I suspected, they turned out to be young seminarians in training at a local Bible college. Eagerly they held their Bibles in their hands and waited triumphantly for me to answer.

Usually, I do not like to debate controversial matters in a public forum, for fear of stirring combative natures, but there seemed no way to avoid dealing with these ministerial students. Anyway, they had my path completely blocked, and the circle of listeners looked at me expectantly for some explanation.

"Well, it seems as though you have studied the subject of the covenants quite deeply," I suggested.

"Oh, yes," they affirmed, "we know all about the covenants."

"Good," I replied. "You undoubtedly know when the Old Covenant was instituted." One of them spoke up quickly, "It was started at Mt. Sinai."

"And how was it ratified?" I asked. Without a moment's hesitation one of them answered, "By the sprinkling of the blood of an ox."

"Very good," I commented, "and how

was the New Covenant ratified?" All three chorused the answer, "By the blood of Jesus on the cross."

I commended the young men for their knowledge of the Scriptures and asked them to read me two verses out of their own Bibles—Hebrews 9:16, 17 and Galatians 3:15. They responded eagerly to the invitation, and read the verses, commenting on each one after reading. "We agree that the New Covenant did not go into effect until after Christ died, and nothing can be added or taken away after He ratified it on the cross," the spokesman for the group asserted. All three nodded their heads emphatically over this point.

I said, "Now you must answer two more questions for me. Here's the first one, and you must think carefully to give me the correct answer: When did Sunday-keeping begin?" There was a moment of shocked silence, and then another, and another. The boys looked at each other, and then down at their feet, and then back at me. I gently prodded them for the answer, "Surely you can tell me the answer to this question. You have known all the others, and have answered correctly. When and why do you think people began keeping Sunday?"

Finally, one of them said, "We keep Sunday in honor of the resurrection of Jesus." I said, "Then I must ask you my last question. How could Sundaykeeping be a part of the New Covenant? You just stated that nothing could be added after the death of Christ. He died on Friday and was resurrected on Sunday. If Sunday was added after Jesus died, it could never be a part of the New Covenant, could it?"

The three young men shuffled their feet, looked helplessly around, and one of them said, "We'll study into that and talk to you later." Then they fled from that auditorium as fast as they could go. I can assure you, also, that they never returned to talk further about the covenants.

The fact is that Sundaykeeping, even if it had started on the day of the resurrection, would have been three days too late to get into the New Covenant. Both Bible and history prove that Sunday was never observed by the apostolic church. It was added much, much later as a result of the gradual apostasy which developed in the early centuries of the church and which culminated in the pagan accommodation of Constantine in 330 A.D.

Millions of modern church members regard Sunday as a sacred day which memorializes the resurrection of Christ. It is certainly true that Christ arose on the first day of the week, but nowhere in the Bible are we commanded to keep that day holy. Events such as the crucifixion and resurrection should mean much to every Christian, but not one intimation is given in the Bible for observing either Friday or Sunday. The only day ever commanded for weekly worship is the seventh day of the week—the same Sabbath Jesus kept during creation week and the one He will keep with His people throughout all eternity. Genesis 2:1-3; Isaiah 66:22, 23.

The very strongest reason for rejecting Sunday worship is that it was not included in the New Covenant requirements which were ratified by the death of Jesus. If Christ had desired His resurrection to be memorialized by Sundaykeeping, He could have introduced it on that same Thursday night of the Last Supper. Then it would have become a part of the New Covenant, along with the Communion service and foot-washing. Jesus did not hesitate to command the observance of His death, even though it had not taken place yet. Just as easily He could have commanded the observance of His resurrection, which was still future, in order that it might become a New Covenant requirement. *But He did not!* And no one else ever did either, until Paul's prophecy began to be fulfilled about an apostasy following his departure. Acts 20:29, 30. He spoke also of a falling away which would lead to the enthronement of Antichrist. 2 Thessalonians 2:3, 4. But true it is that no hint of any change of the law is given in the Scriptures. The unchangeable moral law was preserved in both Old and New Covenants as the perfect revelation of God's will.

Ishmael and Isaac
Represent Two Covenants

With this background, we are now prepared to examine Galatians 4. Many have been confused over the allegory Paul used to illustrate the Old and New Covenants. Here is the way he wrote about it: "For it is written, that Abraham had two sons, the one by a bondmaid, the other by a freewoman. But he who was of the bondwoman was born after the flesh; but he of the freewoman was by promise. Which things are an allegory: for these are the two covenants; the one from the mount Sinai, which gendereth to bondage, which is Agar. For this Agar is mount Sinai in Arabia, and answereth to Jerusalem which now is, and is in bondage with her children." Verses 22-25.

Paul portrays Isaac and Ishmael, the two sons of Abraham, as representing the Old and New Covenants. He plainly shows that Hagar's son, Ishmael, symbolizes the Old Covenant, and Sarah's son, Isaac, is a type of the New Covenant. "Now we, brethren,

as Isaac was, are the children of promise. ...
So then, brethren, we are not children of
the bondwoman, but of the free." Verses
28-31.

This is interesting. How do those sons
of those two women represent the two
covenants? Actually, they are a perfect
illustration according to everything we have
learned so far. God had promised Abraham
a son by his wife Sarah, but because she
was almost 90 years old, neither of them
believed such a thing could happen. Sarah
knew that her womb was dead and that she
was long past the age for bearing children.
So she suggested that her husband take
Hagar, her handmaid, and have a child by
her. It seemed the only way to rescue God
from an impossible promise. In time,
Abraham yielded to the face-saving device
and had a child by Hagar.

Here is an exact illustration of the Old
Covenant principle of "we will do."
Abraham tried to work it out in the flesh,
according to human effort and planning.
The old arrangement failed just as surely as
the Old Covenant promises failed, because

there was no dependence on divine power. God did not ever recognize Ishmael as the promised seed.

When Isaac was born, it was a miracle. God actually created a new life out of a biologically barren womb. The physical impossibilities yielded to the supernatural, creative power of God. Isaac perfectly represents the principle of the New Covenant relationship based upon regeneration, a new-birth experience, which begets the life of the Son of God in all who believe. The natural, physical womb of Sarah was totally incapable of producing any fruit. In the same way, the natural, carnal body and mind of a sinner cannot bring forth the fruit of obedience. When God used His power to create a new life within Sarah, the impossible happened, and she bore a son. When God uses His power to create new life in the soul, the impossible happens again—a human being becomes spiritual and obedient.

Isaac was not "born after the flesh," but "after the Spirit." Galatians 4:29. Because man is carnal and "weak in the flesh," he has no power to attain to the righteousness of the law. He, too, must be born after the Spirit. Every attempt to obey on the Old-Covenant basis of human effort will produce only children of bondage. The law must be written into the heart by the Holy Spirit and fulfilled by "Christ in you."

This allegory of Hagar and Sarah clears up another very important point of truth. Those who are under the Old Covenant are the commandment breakers, and those under the New Covenant are the commandment keepers. It was only when Abraham disobeyed God by taking Hagar that he fulfilled the principle of the Old Covenant. When he trusted God to give him a son through Sarah, he was being obedient to God's will, and properly represents the New-Covenant Christians. Yet how often do modern interpreters get these facts confused! Like the three young preachers, they accuse law-keepers of being under the Old Covenant. The truth is exactly the opposite. The law is not really kept until it is written on the heart of the transformed believer. Then it becomes the mark of identification—

the love symbol—for those who are born of the Spirit. Jesus said, "If ye love me, keep my commandments." John 14:15. John wrote, "For this is the love of God, that we keep his commandments." 1 John 5:3.

True Circumcision is Not Physical

Have you ever wondered why God gave circumcision to Abraham as a sign of the Old Covenant? Doesn't that seem to be a rather crude way to represent such an important agreement? Think about it for a moment and it might begin to make a lot of sense. God gave Abraham the sign of circumcision to remind him of how he failed by trusting the flesh. All through the Scriptures, physical circumcision is related to dependence on the flesh. Paul wrote, "For we are the circumcision, which worship God in the spirit, and rejoice in Christ Jesus, and have no confidence in the flesh." Philippians 3:3.

Paul was comparing true circumcision with "that which is called circumcision." The cutting off of the flesh was not true circumcision at all: "For he is not a Jew, which is one outwardly; neither is that circumcision, which is outward in the flesh: But he is a Jew, which is one inwardly; and circumcision is that of the heart, in the spirit, and not in the letter; whose praise is not of men, but of God." Romans 2:28, 29. Notice how Paul turns from the flesh to the Spirit. He says real circumcision happens to the heart, and it exalts what God does, and not man. It is the cutting off of the fleshly nature through conversion. The new birth is the true circumcision experience.

The clearest explanation is found in Paul's epistle to the Colossians: "In whom also ye are circumcised with the circumcision made without hands, in putting off the body of the sins of the flesh by the circumcision of Christ." Colossians 2:11.

Here the spiritual work of Christ on the heart is called circumcision. It is done without hands, indicating that no human effort could perform this act. It is not cutting off the physical flesh, but cutting off the fleshly nature of sin through the indwelling of Christ. It will be available to all on exactly the same basis: "And if ye be Christ's, then are ye Abraham's seed, and heirs according to the promise." Galatians 3:29. All who receive Christ become heirs of all the promises made to Abraham. Those experiencing true heart-circumcision constitute the real Jews.

No longer can anyone boast of belonging to the right physical family. There is no more Jew or Gentile, male or female. Acceptance is based upon personal faith in Jesus Christ as Saviour. Neither can any man claim special favor for cutting off the physical foreskin of flesh. Those things were done by people who based everything on "we will do." They sought justification and salvation through works of the flesh. God's new plan through Christ is not of works, but of grace through faith.

Does this mean that works are no longer important? Since the law cannot justify, should it be abolished by the believer? The doctrine of the covenants establishes beyond any doubt that the law is just as important under the New as under the Old. Instead of being graven on stone, it is written in the heart. Instead of being fulfilled by us, it is fulfilled by Jesus in us. Instead of keeping the law in order to be saved, we keep it because we are saved. The same works of obedience are there, but they are there for a different reason and from a different motive.

Sometimes, without realizing it, we can begin to trust our traditional round of religious exercises far more than we ought. No merit system must clog the free channels of faith, love, and grace. Obedience in its proper position is important and necessary, but it must always be in that position— following grace and accompanied by love.

In fact, it is possible to put ourselves back under the Old Covenant even today if we begin to trust our works to save us. Just as the saints of old could have received true circumcision by accepting spiritual regeneration, we may fall back under the Old Covenant by trusting the flesh to save us.